An Unlikely Leader

Written by Kerrie Shanahan

Illustrated by Lyn Stone

Flying Start
to Literacy®

Contents

Prologue

My heart was beating fast and loud. I could hear it thudding in my ears. My mouth was dry. My breathing short. And butterflies raced around in my stomach.

How did I get myself into this situation? How can I, 12-year-old Mitchell Whitmore, be about to speak at the Glenville City Council meeting in front of a roomful of adults?

Maybe I can just leave? No one will notice!

My eyes darted around, looking for the closest exit.

"Ready, Mitch?" The gentle voice immediately snapped my thoughts back to the present. My escape plan was put on hold . . . for a moment.

I pasted a brave smile on my face. "Yes, Iris."

Iris smiled back at me. She squeezed my hand.

You can do this, Mitchell Whitmore, I told myself.
You can do this!

I took some slow, deep breaths as I reflected on how I came to be there . . .

Chapter 1

Bad news

As the school bell rang, we all spilled out of
the building.

"Mitchell! Over here!" It was my best friend, Zack.

Zack and I had lived on the same street our whole lives.
We walked home together every afternoon.

"Can you go to the park on the way home?" Zack asked.

It was more like a woodland than a park, and we loved
stopping there on our way home from school. It was a small
patch of nature in the middle of our hot, cement-filled city.

"Sure can. Race you!" I said.

In no time, we were in the middle of tall trees, grasses and
shrubs. There were birds calling to one another, grasshoppers
chirping and butterflies flitting around in the sunlight.

"Hey, Mitch, check this out!" I followed Zack's gaze up to
the fork in a cedar tree. It was a bird's nest. *Cool!*

A bird with golden feathers on its face looked at us from
its nest.

"Wow! I've never seen one of those before."

I was a bit of a bird "expert" and knew most of the bird
species in our woodland park. I got out my notebook and
did a quick sketch, making a mental note to search for
information on this bird when I got home.

Later, as Zack and I left the park, we noticed a sign.

"What's this all about?" My brain slowly processed the
words: *Planning Notice!*
Tenpin Bowling Alley Coming Soon . . .

"No!" A small gasp escaped from my mouth.

"What does it mean?" Zack was confused.

"It means they're putting in a proposal to redevelop the park. They want to *develop* the area and build a tenpin bowling alley here."

"How can they do that?" said Zack. "How can they just knock down the trees and change the park? It's not fair!"

"We can't let it happen!" I said.

When I got home, I told Dad about the sign.

"That's a shame," he said. "But you like bowling, don't you?"

I looked at Dad. *Is he serious? Doesn't he get it?*

I decided that I'd talk to Mum about it. She'd know what to do!

"When's Mum getting home?" I asked.

"She has a late meeting tonight." My dad had his head in a recipe book. "But she said she'll see you and your sister at breakfast tomorrow."

I guessed I'd have to wait until morning.

Breakfast time the following morning was crazy.

"Mummm," my sister, Bella, bellowed. "Where are my soccer shoes?"

"Out on the porch!" Mum yelled back as she stuffed a pile of papers in her bag. She took a big sip of coffee and stepped into her shiny high-heeled shoes. She searched for her car keys, grabbed a piece of toast and gave us all a quick kiss goodbye.

"Have a great day everyone."

"Mum, I need to talk . . ."

The door banged, and she was gone. My mum's job was hectic. She always had meetings and paperwork and presentations. She was so busy . . . I figured I'd just have to talk to her that night.

"Are you two ready?" Dad's deep voice was calm. If Mum was a tornado, then Dad was a still summer's day. Steady. Quiet. Kind. Everyone says I'm just like him, even though Mum is kind, too!

"We need to go!" Bella commanded. She was just like Mum. Always busy. I called her bossy, but my mum said she had *leadership skills.*

"I have soccer before school," Bella informed us. "I can't be late, Dad. I'm the captain, you know!"

Dad and I looked at each other knowingly.

Chapter 2

A plan goes wrong

I couldn't stop thinking about the park redevelopment all day at school. Luckily, when I got home after school, Mum was there. Finally, I could talk to her.

"Mum, I need to talk to you about something."

"Sure, Mitch," Mum said, with a smile that lit up the room. "Have you decided to run for student leader?" Mum snuck this in before I could speak. I groaned inwardly.

"Mum, you know I'm not a leader," I shrugged. "I hate talking in front of people, and no one would want to listen to my ideas."

"That's not true, Mitchell John! You'd be great. It'd be a terrific experience." And she flashed that smile again.

"Okay. I'll think about it." But I knew it wasn't for me.

"Your sister loved being class captain." Mum just wouldn't let up and now I was annoyed.

"I'm not Bella!" I snapped.

"I know! I know! Sorry . . . just think about it. What did you want to talk about?"

"Doesn't matter." I was sulky and didn't feel like chatting anymore.

"Okay then. Next time. I have to go, Mitch. I have a work thing to get to." Mum jumped up from her seat and whirled out the door.

I sighed. I would just have to come up with my own plan to save the park. And I did!

I decided to hold a meeting at school. If the other kids found out what was going to happen to the park, they'd want to do something to stop it.

So I got busy putting together a flyer on the computer in Dad's office. Soon, I had printed a big pile of flyers to hand out at school the next day.

It looked like I didn't need Mum and Dad's help after all. Imagine how proud they would be when I saved the park!

Save Glenville's Park

The trees in our beautiful park are going to be chopped down!

If you disagree, then let's do something about it!

Meet me at lunchtime in the schoolyard.

Mitch Whitmore

The next morning, I handed out the flyers as everyone walked into school. At lunchtime, Zack and I raced out to the schoolyard. We were excited to see who would come and what ideas they had.

We waited and waited. *Where is everyone?*

After 20 minutes, it was clear that no one was coming. *Why aren't they interested?*

"Maybe we should just drop it," said Zack sadly.

"We can't!" I sounded certain, but I wasn't sure, either.

The next day after school, Zack didn't want to go to the park.

"Sorry," he said, and kept walking while looking at
the ground.

I walked alone into the heart of the park.

"Hello there." I turned and saw our next-door neighbour, Iris.
"Come and see some baby birds," she said excitedly.

Iris walked briskly ahead of me. She knew lots about nature and I loved listening to her. She stopped and pointed up into a tree at two nestlings.

"There," she said. It was the same nest Zack and I had seen.

"Oh wow!" I was captivated. "I saw a bird in that nest earlier this week. I was going to do some research about it, but I forgot. I'll do it when I get home."

"Well, let me know what you find out," said Iris. Then the look in her eyes turned serious. "Did you hear there's a proposal to build here? On this land?"

I nodded.

"This can't happen!" She sounded determined. "Maybe you and your school friends could help me stop it?"

"I've tried that," I said glumly. "No one's interested."

"Oh, that's a shame." Iris looked sad.

And we walked home together, lost in our own thoughts.

Chapter 3
A surprise discovery

When I got home, I went straight to the computer. I searched for information about the yellow-faced bird I had seen in the park. What I found out amazed me!

I printed the information and ran next door.

I burst into Iris's kitchen. "Iris," I said, "look what I found out. The bird I saw is called a Golden-cheeked Warbler. It's only found in our state, and it's an endangered species!"

Iris scanned the information.

"Are you sure this was the bird you saw?" She looked doubtful.

"I'm positive!" And I showed Iris the sketch I had done.

"We need a photo." Iris sprang into action. "Can you take one?"

"Ummm." I hesitated.

"Mitchell, this is important. Here."

She thrust her camera into my hands.

"Now, I need to make some calls. And Mitch, you'll need to come to a meeting with me tonight and tell everyone about the Golden-cheeked Warbler you saw." Iris was on a mission.

"What meeting?" I asked.

"Don't worry about the details. I'll contact your dad and tell him about it. Now, go and get that photo!"

I raced home to tell Dad where I was going.

"Dad, I need to dash back to the park and take a photo of a bird."

"What? A bird? What bird?" Dad was confused.

"It's too hard to explain, but it's important."

"Okay then." Dad wasn't sure what was happening, but he trusted me. "Don't be long. We have Bella's musical tonight."

Oh no! The musical! I'd forgotten all about it.

"You know Bella has the lead role," Dad continued. "We can't miss it."

"But . . . but . . . Iris wants me to go to a meeting with her. It's about the bird. She's going to call you and explain."

"No buts. Mum can't go to the musical. She's got an emergency work meeting, so it's just you and me. Now you'd better take that photo, before it's too late."

I zipped out the door and straight back to the same tree. I craned my neck to see the nest. I waited and waited.

Hurry up, bird. Iris really needs this photo!

Then I heard a high-pitched birdsong. It was the golden-faced bird! I aimed the camera and clicked. *Click. Click. Click.* I checked to be sure I had a clear shot. *Yes!*

I ran all the way back home to print the photos, and then rushed over to Iris's house to show her.

"I got it," I said breathlessly, "but I can't go to the meeting. I have to go to Bella's performance."

"I spoke to your dad, and he agrees with us," said Iris. He wants us to go to the meeting and fight for what we believe in!"

Chapter 4
The meeting

So, that's how I ended up at the council meeting – as nervous as I'd ever been in my life!

"Let's get started." The mayor's voice was full of authority. The buzz of chatter died down and all eyes turned towards the mayor.

As I looked up, I saw a familiar figure out of the corner of my eye. I looked again. It was Mum! *Dad must have told her about everything. She's come to support me . . . instead of watching Bella.* With Mum in the audience, I was suddenly confident to talk about protecting the park.

"We're here to discuss the development of the Glenville Park area," said the mayor. "The Biggs Corporation will present its plans. Then the public can respond."

"Let's welcome Meredith Whitmore from Biggs."

Meredith Whitmore? That's my mum's name.

I sat numbly as I watched Mum walk to the front of the room. What was she *doing*?

She flashed her smile and began her presentation: a professional slide show full of shiny photos and an artist's drawings. *"Sustainable design. Modern facilities. Family friendly. Fun, social activity . . ."*

These phrases rolled easily off my mum's tongue. She had the audience eating out of her hand. I was in shock! How could Mum want this?

When she finished, the mayor asked for comments.

Iris stood up.

"You should not agree with this proposal," she said passionately.

She spoke about the need for trees – to filter the air, reduce pollution, and provide shade and a home for animals. And she spoke about the community needing a place to enjoy nature.

"Now, Mayor, can you show the photo I sent you?" Iris asked.

The photo I took of the Golden-cheeked Warbler flashed onto the screen.

Then Iris introduced me . . .

You can do this, Mitchell Whitmore, I told myself. *You can do this!*

Shakily, I stood up and began talking about the bird I had discovered. I started nervously, but as I spoke, I warmed up. I knew that what I was saying was important.

"Golden-cheeked Warblers were once abundant in this area. Now they are endangered because we keep destroying their homes. But these birds are nesting here, in our park! This is massive news. We cannot cut down this endangered bird's home!"

My cheeks glowed as the audience clapped. I looked for Mum, but I couldn't see her.

Chapter 5
The fight continues

Iris drove me home, and I ran up the front stairs two at a time. I couldn't wait to tell Dad. But someone had beaten me to it. Mum and Dad were sitting at the kitchen table deep in conversation.

"Mitch!" Dad was excited. "I'm so proud of you!"

"Thanks, Dad. But why didn't you tell me it was Mum's project?"

"I didn't know." Dad shrugged.

"I had to fill in for Alan at the last minute," Mum explained. "Our company is so big, I wasn't even aware of this development until today. Why didn't you tell me about *your* views?"

"I tried, Mum, but you were too busy."

"I'm sorry, Mitch," she said.

And then we all laughed. It was pretty odd, both of us speaking at a council meeting!

"Well," said Dad, "we'll have to wait and see who wins."

"That's right," said Mum. "You and Iris put up some good arguments, but it's not over yet."

"By the way, Mum. I've decided not to go for student leader." I thought it was as good a time as any to tell her.

"Don't worry about that," Mum said. "What you did tonight showed great leadership! Besides, I have a feeling you're going to be too busy."

"What do you mean?"

"You'll find out." Mum looked like she knew something I didn't.

Mum was right. After that night, I became really busy.

First of all, a journalist interviewed me. He used the photos I had taken for his article about the park and the birds, and the development proposal. The story was on the front page of our local newspaper.

Then my school principal asked me to talk at assembly about the whole issue. The kids seemed really interested, and they clapped loudly at the end of my talk. Some of the classes even wrote letters to the city council about saving the park and the Golden-cheeked Warblers.

And then my teacher suggested that Zack and I start a nature group. This time, lots of kids were interested in the idea and joined the group.

Our nature group organised a clean-up day at the park. We put notices about it in the school newsletter and stuffed flyers in letterboxes. Iris arranged for a local nursery to donate native trees for us to plant. Lots of people came, and Bella's soccer team ran a sausage sizzle for all the volunteers. The mayor even came and helped. It was a great day.

You know the saying: "From little things big things grow?" Well, I guess that's what happened here!

One month later . . .

One hot day, when I arrived home from school, Iris was sitting at the kitchen table with Dad. As I opened the door, they both jumped out of their seats.

"Mitch! We won! The proposal has been denied," Iris said.

"Yes," added Dad, "the council said that the birds need to be protected."

"Plus," continued Iris, "the mayor said that the community needs the park. It's too special to get rid of."

I couldn't get a word in, so I just smiled.

Later that night when Mum got home, she was in a cheery mood.

"Mitch!" she said, beaming. "I heard the news. Congratulations!" And she gave me a big bear hug.

"Thanks, Mum," I said. "I hope everything's okay with your work."

"It's the right decision. We should have done our research better."

If Mum was disappointed, she didn't show it.

"Besides," Mum continued, "the council has put aside money in its budget to improve the park so that more people visit. The council needs a company to design the improvements. We could have a boardwalk and an information centre, and also clean up the stream and plant trees to encourage birdlife. What do you think?"

"Sounds good to me!" I said. And it did.

A note from the author

When we think of leaders, we usually think of strong, loud, confident people who are great public speakers.

In this story, I wanted the hero to be a different type of leader – someone who leads by being intelligent, thoughtful and passionate. And so I began to develop the character of Mitchell. He wasn't overly confident and didn't see himself as a leader, but because he cared so much about the issue, he ended up fighting hard for it and winning!

I also thought it would be a good twist in the plot to have Mitchell's mum working for the company that was redeveloping the woodland park. Members of a family often have differing opinions about issues, so I thought this would add an interesting layer to the story.

I hope Mitchell inspires you to become a leader and stand up for what you believe in!